ONE BIBLE, ONE MESSAGE

One Bible, One Message?

Common Mistakes about the Bible

Bryan A. Williams

EVANGELICAL PRESS OF WALES

© Evangelical Press of Wales, 1989
First published 1989
ISBN 1 85049 069 4

Cover design: Vincent McDonnell

Published by the Evangelical Press of Wales
Bryntirion, Bridgend, Mid Glamorgan CF31 4DX, Wales
Printed by Bath Press

Contents

Introduction

In this little book we are going to look at some errors that are prevalent about the Bible, mistakes with which Christians are often faced and which can cause them a great deal of trouble and distress.

Let us emphasize at once that what we have in mind is not mistakes *in* the Bible, but mistakes *about* the Bible. Such errors sometimes arise from shallow study of the Scriptures, from a failure properly to relate the different parts. In other cases the errors are the result of false instruction. Two centuries of negative and sceptical criticism have left their mark!

In particular, errors have become widespread in one central area: *the relation of the Old Testament to the New Testament*. The Christian Bible is treated by many as if it were two separable parts, the first being obsolete ('Was it ever applicable to the church anyway?' some ask) and the second being more or less binding upon the Christian.

The following brief and non-technical study seeks to examine some key areas of error.

1
Are the Old and New Testaments equally reliable?

Is the Bible historically and theologically accurate? May we trust the Old and New Testaments equally? Is the Bible's authority limited to matters of faith and practice? Does it matter whether or not we accept the Scriptures as trustworthy in every respect?

Each of these questions raises a further question, namely: Is there a sound criterion by which any Christian can examine or assess the conflicting answers that some church leaders and theologians give to these questions?

What kinds of statements do we regard as reliable? Surely those that are spoken or written by someone whose character and knowledge are worthy of trust. In other words, reliability depends upon the integrity and authority of the speaker or writer responsible for the message. Who then is responsible for the Old and New Testaments?

The Old Testament in many places records the words of *God*. It is he who spoke to Adam and Eve in the Garden of Eden. He spoke to Adam and Eve's sons,

Cain and Abel. He made himself known regularly to Enoch. To Noah he gave his assessment of the state of mankind and news of impending judgment. From time to time God spoke to Abraham, giving him wonderful promises for the future. And so on. God revealed himself and his ways to patriarch, lawgiver, priest, judge, king and prophet. In the Authorized Version of the Bible, again and again we read in the books of the prophets: 'Thus saith the Lord . . .' Expressions like 'The word of the Lord came to me' appear ten times in the first twenty verses of Jeremiah. Ezekiel reports hearing God's message scores of times.

There is no doubt that the Old Testament books were regarded as God-given and therefore reliable, and binding on their readers in every area of their lives. This is obvious, for instance, in Leviticus. There is nothing theoretical about the cultic, ceremonial and hygienic regulations there. Similarly, the word of a judge or prophet (themselves inspired by God) was given to be obeyed. From the numerous examples, we can refer to the record of Samuel's life and words, or illustrate the same point from the call of Jonah to the people of Nineveh to repent before God. In the Psalms a climax is reached in Psalm 119, which in almost every verse refers to God's command or decree or the like. In verse 105 the psalmist declares:

> Your word is a lamp to my feet
> and a light for my path.

The same note of Old Testament reliability, based on God's character and command, is sounded in the New Testament. Jesus' teaching on the subject is as forthright as it can possibly be. In the Sermon on the Mount he is constantly underlining the authority of the Old Testament.

Do not think that I have come to abolish the Law or the Prophets; I have not come to abolish them but to fulfil them. *I tell you the truth, until heaven and earth disappear, not the smallest letter, not the least stroke of a pen, will by any means disappear from the Law until everything is accomplished.* Anyone who breaks one of the least of these commandments and teaches others to do the same will be called least in the kingdom of heaven, but whoever practises and teaches these commands will be called great in the kingdom of heaven (Matthew 5:17-19).

In the passage quoted, only 'the Law' and 'the Prophets' are mentioned, but in a remarkable talk after his resurrection, Jesus included the whole Old Testament, referring to it in the traditional Jewish way by the threefold designation 'the Law of Moses, the Prophets and the Psalms' (Luke 24:44). More than that, he declared that everything in these sources concerning him '*must be fulfilled*'. The Old Testament was still valid for Jesus. Indeed, he seems deliberately to have anticipated modern doubts as to the reliability of the Old Testament by carefully endorsing some of the seemingly incredible parts (see Matthew 12:39-41).

The confidence placed in the Old Testament by the New Testament authors was boundless. Matthew was apparently never happier than when writing triumphantly: 'And so was fulfilled what the Lord had said through the prophet . . .' (This statement, with unimportant variations, appears a number of times in the first Gospel even before the end of chapter 2.) John quotes from the Old Testament only about twenty times, but his book is steeped in imagery from it. Romans, Paul's spiritual and intellectual masterpiece on God's righteousness and man's need of salvation met in Christ, is built firmly on seventy texts from the Old Testament.

Hebrews is so heavily dependent on it that it would be meaningless apart from an acquaintance with the Old Testament. The writer treats the Old Testament writings as a 'mashal', a parable which waits for an explanation. The explanations given in Hebrews are that Old Testament passages are types or fore-shadowings of Christ and the gospel. The Old Testament is the age of anticipation awaiting the age of fulfilment. This is seen in respect of the 'rest' spoken of first in the wilderness period (Hebrews 3:18), then in David's day (Hebrews 4:3), then at the time when the Epistle was written (Hebrews 4:5-10). The same historical perspective is seen in chapter 11.

Much of the argument of Hebrews is based on quotations from the Psalms — Psalms 2, 8, 40, 45, 95, 102, 104, 110. Five or six of these Psalms are quoted in the first chapter alone. Often a part of a Psalm is quoted and then expounded. Sometimes the Psalm quotation is followed by another Old Testament passage on the same theme — e.g. in Hebrews 6:20ff., Psalm 110 is followed by references to the Genesis 14 narrative, and this in turn leads on to the exposition on the subject of the priesthood of Melchizedek.

2 Timothy 3:16-17 says it all: '*All Scripture is God-breathed* and is useful for teaching, rebuking, correcting and training in righteousness, so that the man of God may be thoroughly equipped for every good work.' Now, in context, the 'Scripture' concerned is the *Old* Testament, the only written sacred collection of works in the very early New Testament church. We see, too, that men are only secondary authors. *God* is the primary author, who has not *in*spired the words of human be-

ings, but *ex*pired (= breathed out) his word through them, while not suppressing their distinctive personalities and past experiences.

In fact the emerging New Testament is regarded as having authority because the Old has, rather than the other way round. This seems to be the force of 2 Peter 1:19 — 'And we have the word of the prophets made more certain' — though not all English versions render it in this way.

In 1 Timothy 5:18 a verse from the Old Testament (Deuteronomy 25:4) is immediately followed by one from the New Testament (Luke 10:7): both are introduced by the formula, 'the Scripture says'. And in 2 Peter 3:16, Paul's books are highly praised with the words that unstable people distort them 'as they do *the other Scriptures*' (= the Old Testament).

For many the reliability of the *New* Testament hardly needs emphasizing. Much of the Gospels consists of Jesus' own words. Sometimes, as in the Sermon on the Mount (Matthew, chapters 5 to 7), or in the Upper Room teaching recorded by John (chapters 14 to 16, together with the prayer in chapter 17), there are lengthy passages of direct speech uttered by the Lord. The narrative parts of the Gospels are written by disciples of Jesus or their disciples. So are the Acts and the Epistles, which on occasion include statements from the Master (see Acts 9; 1 Corinthians 11:23-25). Nevertheless, the authenticity of the New Testament has been questioned seriously and repeatedly by some scholars in recent generations, and therefore, even in so short a book as this, we must face several questions. It seems best to do so here, before concluding this chapter.

How do we know that the words attributed to Jesus really are his own? One answer is that at least *some* passages are accepted by the most sceptical critics. Thus,

13

even Rudolf Bultmann acknowledged about forty sayings as genuinely from Jesus. Another answer — which is very potent — is that only outstanding individuals utter memorable statements like those of the Jesus presented in the Gospels. Communities or committees (often given the credit, by the more radical New Testament scholars, for Gospel speeches) never do. Thirdly, the historical argument is very important. The early church was extremely vigilant about its books. Paul refers in one letter to living witnesses to the resurrected Jesus (1 Corinthians 15). One fragment of John's Gospel, called the John Rylands Papyrus, goes back to within perhaps twenty-five years of the date of the completion of the Gospel itself. Thus the church *accepted* books it believed true. Conversely, it *rejected* other so-called Gospels — perhaps as many as fifty that emerged in the first four or five centuries. Very early on, Luke reflects the discriminating attitude of the church regarding authentic and false reports of the life and teaching of Jesus (Luke 1:1-4).

Can we trust the words attributed to Jesus, even if we admit them to be authentic? The answer here is 'Yes!' Yes on historical, archaeological and linguistic grounds, but still more on *personal* grounds. The Christian is a person who is indwelt by the Holy Spirit. That Spirit who inspired Scripture (2 Timothy 3:16; 2 Peter 1:21) testifies to the reality of spiritual life in the believer (Romans 8:16-17; 1 John 2:20), and enlightens and convicts him regarding the truth of Scripture (John 14:26, 16:13). The writers testify to Jesus' uniqueness — to his sinlessness, indeed, to his divine Sonship — and an answering chord vibrates in the Christian. We need to study passages such as John 1:1-18, Philippians 2:5-11, John 10:35-36 and Hebrews 1:8 very carefully indeed. We trust Jesus' words because of Jesus' Person, and because of the historical and personal testimony of the Spirit to both.

Granted that the words attributed to Jesus are trustworthy, may we place the same confidence in the remainder of the New Testament, or indeed the Old Testament? Is the Bible *wholly* reliable? Various approaches have been adopted. Some, for instance, will accept the Gospels as a historical record, but not certain Old Testament books, such as Jonah or Esther. Others will accept the general value of Scripture, that is, the religious thoughts it contains, but not the very words that express those thoughts. For such, reliability may be restricted to 'theological' material, while it may be denied to historical material. Against these assaults there are several convincing lines of defence.

Firstly, there is the demonstrable consistency and harmony of the Bible. One area must suffice as an example, namely the giving of prophecy and its fulfilment. Especially important in this respect, of course, are those prophecies relating to Christ, where the detailed realization of the prophecies is nothing short of astounding.

Further, it is significant to note that many references previously questioned have been confirmed, notably, but not exclusively, in the realm of archaeology. Very much evidence has come to light over the last hundred years verifying biblical material. Patriarchal customs described in Genesis have been seen to accord perfectly with the picture derived from the Middle East in the period 2000-1700 BC. The Tell-el-Amana tablets discovered in Egypt in 1887 apparently refer to the Israelite invasion of Palestine. Luke's Gospel and his second book, Acts, have been shown to display a previously undreamed-of level of accuracy regarding things such as official Roman titles and places. An astonishing about-turn has taken place over the last fifty years concerning the attention to detail in John's Gospel. So great is this that the expression 'new look' has come into common use to denote the change of attitude brought about through the Dead Sea Scrolls and other newly discovered documents.

Most importantly, however, it is the character of God that demands a consistently true Bible. In both Testaments, God is represented as speaking hundreds of times. He is the Revealer (Hebrews 1:2). He is the Almighty (Psalm 91:1). He is ethically perfect (1 Peter 1:16; compare with Leviticus 11:44, 19:2; 1 John 1:5). Thus he has the will and power to reveal truth, and to *preserve* truth through the ages. He will not mislead. The Scriptures are reliable because God is reliable. How could the God of the Bible, the perfect Trinity of Father, Son and Spirit, the God Christians trust implicitly for his uprightness and holiness, give a faulty revelation of himself and his ways? If he did, it would be a kind of celestial teasing to leave us with a revelation permeated with error, and one, moreover, where we could never be sure where the error was to be found.

There is, of course, a difference between the teaching of Jesus and that of the Old Testament. He seems to intensify the demands of the Ten Commandments, for instance, in Matthew 5:21-28. Yet does he *really* do so? The evil *attitude* as well as the outward sinful acts must alike be prohibited by the all-embracing first commandment and the tenth commandment. The first demands uncompromised loyalty to God, while the other specifically covers *attitudes*, and not just the *acts* that stem from them. In other passages Jesus does not dispense with the Old Testament, *but roundly condemns the use the Jewish teachers made of it*. Especially is this seen to be true in Matthew 23 — see, for example, verses 16 to 24.

In the last chapter of the Bible, two very strong declarations highlight the Lord's authority:

> I warn everyone who hears the words of the prophecy of this book: If anyone adds anything to them, God will add to him the plagues described in this book. And if anyone takes words away from this book of prophecy, God will take away from him his share in the tree of life and in the holy city, which are described in this book (Revelation 22:18-19).

While they apply to Revelation itself in the first place, it can hardly be disputed that they set the seal on the New Testament and the whole Bible.

We conclude that there is nothing to choose between the Testaments according to their own testimony about their reliability. They have the same Author, God. The Old has not been rescinded by the New. In fact their teaching is that they are essentially 'unrescindable'. The difference is in *fulness* and *clarity* of revelation, not in the *accuracy* of it. A wise child does not deny that two plus two equals four when he learns that four plus four equals eight!

2
The mistake about —
God

The notion that the Old Testament reveals God as Judge but that the New Testament shows him as Father goes back a long way. In the mid second century the heretic Marcion taught the doctrine, and he has not lacked followers since. What is the truth?

God *is* Judge in Old Testament times. His judgment fell on individual people. It came upon the first two human beings — and the third! (See Genesis, chapters 3 and 4.) Amon's assassination, recorded in 2 Kings 21:19-23, appears to be God's punishment for his desertion of true religion.

Sometimes God's judgments came upon whole nations. He judged his grumbling people in the wilderness, sending venomous snakes among them (Numbers 21:4-9). He sent a plague upon Israel because of the sin of its leader (2 Samuel 24). Later he condemned Israel and Judah to subjugation and dispersal when they turned from him to idolatry and immorality (2 Kings 17; 24:20—25:21). But it is not only individuals and nations that God judges. The entire inhabited earth was under judgment at the time of the Flood (Genesis 6—9).

Nor does God send only temporal judgments. In the

Old Testament there are pictures of final judgment, judgment beyond death. Isaiah describes the destiny of the godless king of Babylon in unnerving detail (14:9-17). Daniel speaks of many being raised from the dead at the end 'to shame and everlasting contempt' (12:2).

God is Judge in the New Testament too. In an everyday context Jesus said: 'Do not judge, or you too will be judged' (Matthew 7:1). More terribly, he spoke of the gravest consequences for those who perverted the innocent and helpless (Matthew 18:6). He referred to hell, the place of final judgment, where the 'worm' of the tormented 'does not die, and the fire is not quenched' (Mark 9:47-48). In parables he taught of exclusion from the divine presence and of the unfaithful being thrown 'outside, into the darkness, where there will be weeping and gnashing of teeth' (Matthew 25:1-30). This terrifying situation following final judgment is depicted more fully in the second half of Luke 16, the story of the rich man and Lazarus, and summarized bluntly in the verses on the lake of fire in Revelation (20:14-15).

There can be no doubt that the portrayal of eternal judgment is far fuller and more starkly presented in the New Testament than in the Old. If differences of presentation are sought, one is that in the New Testament God is Judge, but has 'entrusted all judgment to the Son' (John 5:22).

No one will dispute that in the New Testament Jesus teaches that God is the Father. He begins the Lord's Prayer with the words 'Our Father'. He assures fearful followers that their 'heavenly Father knows' their needs (see Matthew 6:25-34). In a few verses in John he uses the title 'Father' ten times for God (John 5:16-27). In his high priestly prayer (John 17) the Father's presence is everywhere felt. Yet two points need to be made. In the

19

first place, God is Father to Jesus in a different way from his relation to other people. (Jesus makes a careful distinction in John 20:17.) Jesus is the 'only' Son; we are sons and daughters by adoption (John 1:18; compare John 1:12 and Galatians 4:4-5). Secondly, God is Father only to the believing; he is Judge and not Father to others (2 Corinthians 6:14-18).

God is Father on essentially the same basis in the Old Testament. A close relationship between him and the faithful is required by the record of Enoch's life in Genesis 5 and Hebrews 11, and by the title 'God's friend' given to Abraham three times in the Bible (see, for example, James 2:23). Similarly, God spoke to Moses 'face to face, as a man speaks with his friend' (Exodus 33:11). The same note pervades many of the Psalms.

More specifically, the cry of God's true people — contrasted dramatically with those who are not — is found in Isaiah 63. Part of verse 16 reads:

> You, O Lord, are our Father,
> Our Redeemer from of old.

This declaration is repeated in verse 8 of the following chapter.

It is of course true that direct references to God as Father are much more scarce in the Old Testament. We must admit, too, that there is no direct Old Testament equivalent for the endearing Aramaic word 'Abba' (= Father) of Mark 14:36, Romans 8:15 and Galatians 4:6, although the thought of Psalm 103:13 and Proverbs 3:12 comes very close to it. Nevertheless, two assertions may be made confidently:

> Both Testaments reveal God as Judge.
> Both Testaments reveal God as Father.

3
The mistake about —
the Trinity

The Bible nowhere gives a detailed account of the Trinity, but only the building blocks for such an understanding of God. Many people know this, but go on to think, erroneously, that all the teaching we do have comes from the New Testament. That is not so. How then does the credal statement, 'We believe . . . in the Holy Spirit . . . who with Father and Son is worshipped together and glorified together', relate to the Bible? Are we justified in ascribing deity to the Son and to the Spirit?

What does the Old Testament say about the Son of God?

There are what scholars call 'theophanies' — that is, appearances of God to men. In Genesis 18 the record of a remarkable confrontation occurs. Near the start of the chapter we are told simply: 'Abraham looked up and saw three men standing nearby.' A little later we see that two 'men' went on to Sodom (compare 18:22 with 19:1), but Abraham remained 'before the Lord'. Some ancient authorities actually render it: 'but the Lord remained standing before Abraham'. Many consider that 'the Lord' was God's Son. Psalm 110 speaks of *two* 'Lords' — Father and Son. The Hebrew general, Joshua, found himself face to face with the awesome 'commander of the army of the Lord' who accepted his worship as of right (Joshua 5:13-15).

In one of the most memorable and exalted passages in the Bible we learn that Isaiah 'saw the Lord seated on a throne' (Isaiah 6:1). In John's Gospel, Jesus is solemnly identified with that 'Lord'. 'Isaiah . . . saw Jesus' glory and spoke about him' (John 12:41). When Daniel's three fearless friends were thrust into Nebuchadnezzar's furnace, the emperor saw (according to one rendering) a mysterious protector 'like the Son of God' (Daniel 3:25).

Prophetic passages in the Old Testament about the Son of God are to be numbered in the scores! We select only four. Genesis 3:15 deserves attention because it is the first such prophecy. Although veiled, it is clear to the extent that it indicates some mighty Person capable of vanquishing Satan himself. Christians have always taken the verse as a preview of Christ's restoration of a fallen universe. Psalm 22 is so full of predictions of the sufferings of the Son of God on earth that it is hard to know where to start. The song begins with the cry Jesus uttered when on the cross: 'My God, my God, why have you forsaken me?' It even describes the piercing of hands and feet, a Roman, not Jewish, form of death common only a thousand years later. The writer goes further. He says that the sufferer's garments were divided among his tormentors, and lots cast for his clothing. Isaiah 53 describes Jesus exactly at point after point, as the early Christians realized. (See Acts 8:26-40 and 1 Peter 2:21-25.) A uniquely impressive heavenly figure described by Jesus' favourite title for himself ('Son of Man') is revealed in Daniel 7:13-14. There is no mistaking the identity of this Person, who is shown to be a King eternal and worthy of universal worship. In short, he is divine. He is God's Son.

22

What does the Old Testament say about the Spirit of God?

Not nearly as much information as about the Son is given, but what is said is very clear about his existence, his personality, and his utterly super-human power. He does things that only God can do — therefore he *is* divine.

We do not arrive at the end of the second verse in the Bible before reading that 'the Spirit of God' was active in creation. Nothing we know of demands the power and intelligence of God so much as that. The Spirit is not active in some vague general way in creation, though. He gives *life*. Job cried: 'The Spirit of God has made me' (Job 33:4). He gives skills, as Exodus 31 and the following chapters show so lucidly. (See especially verses 1 to 4.) The Spirit gives — on occasion — almost unbelievable physical power to a man (Judges 13:25, 15:14-15), an act that can equally be credited to the 'Sovereign Lord' (16:28). The Spirit is God! He gives prophetic enabling to the most unlikely man, Saul, changing him fundamentally (1 Samuel 10:6). According to the New Testament, men of God were 'carried along by the Holy Spirit' in the production of the Old Testament like ships with raised sails (the literal meaning of a vivid Greek expression in 2 Peter 1:21).

We have reached the important conclusion that the doctrine of the Trinity could, in its essentials, be derived from the *Old Testament* alone. The three Persons are all there and all portrayed as divine. Three: no more, no less.

The New Testament references to the divine nature of the Son are on the surface in many places. From an embarrassment of riches we select Matthew 1:23 and 11:27; John 1:18, 5:18 and 10:30; Romans 9:5; Hebrews 1:8; and Revelation 3:21 and 22:1. Matthew, quoting Isaiah the prophet, says: '"The virgin will be with child and will give birth to a son, and they will call him Immanuel" — which means, "God with us".' He alone is able to reveal the Father because he is himself God. The Jews understood Jesus to be 'making himself equal with God' (John tells us in chapter 5 of his Gospel) — and he did not disabuse them, but rather reinforced that truth. In John 10 the Greek original will not permit the weak idea that Father and Son are one only in purpose or will. Verse 30 *has* to mean *essentially* one. The natural understanding of the Greek of Romans 9:5 is given in the text, not the marginal notes: 'Christ . . . is God.' Jesus is again called God, this time by the Father himself, in Hebrews 1:8. In the book of Revelation he is seen sharing the throne of God the Father.

The Holy Spirit is presented as God in the New Testament. One of his functions is to convict people of sin (John 16:8). He illumines the people of God concerning vital truth (John 16:13). Indeed, it is through his activity — and only so — that people can enter the kingdom of God (John 3:3-5). He sanctifies believers, making them more and more like the Lord Jesus. In the verse that teaches this, the Spirit is actually given the divine name 'Lord' (2 Corinthians 3:18). It is the Spirit who bestows 'fruit' that is basically characteristic of God alone (Galatians 5:22-23).

We have spent less time on the New Testament than the Old here because the facts are clearer and hardly in dispute. How, then, does the teaching of the two parts of the Bible differ with respect to the Trinity? We have just said that the facts are clearer in the New Testament. What else? The main distinction is that there are passages in the New Testament that unite the three Persons. This kind of passage hardly appears in the Old

24

Testament (except in rare cases such as Genesis 1:26: 'Let *us* make man in *our* image, in *our* likeness'). Among the verses that place Father, Son and Holy Spirit together, special attention must be given to Matthew 28:19-20, the Great Commission. Disciples are to be made and baptized 'in the name of the Father and of the Son and of the Holy Spirit'. In John 14:15-17 the soon-to-be-crucified Jesus intimately associated the three in love, comfort and truth. Peter's first Epistle attributes every spiritual blessing mankind enjoys to the members of the Trinity acting in unison (1 Peter 1:2). 2 Corinthians 13:14 is climactic: 'May the grace of the Lord Jesus Christ, and the love of God, and the fellowship of the Holy Spirit be with you all.'

We must never give the impression that there are three Gods, however. The Bible does not do so. The Jews have always shown sure judgment in recognizing the centrality of Deuteronomy 6:4. It is vital. Three Persons; one God! Difficult? Yes! Scriptural? Most certainly!

4
The mistake about —
the people of God

A reader might say, 'Well, there's no problem about that, anyway! In the Old Testament God's people are the Israelites, and in the New Testament men and women everywhere.'

But is the matter really quite so simple?

To begin with, Genesis shows Abraham as the father of the Israelites or Hebrews. There is no doubt at all that the bulk of the Old Testament from Genesis 12 onwards centres on Abraham's natural descendants, and that other peoples are often introduced only in passing, or as in radical opposition to the God of the Hebrews. No one could deny, then, that the major part of the Old Testament concentrates on God's relation to Israel, with special reference to his blessing and judgments on that nation. The last part of Psalm 147 reads:

> [God] has revealed his word to Jacob,
> his laws and decrees to Israel.
> *He has done this for no other nation;*
> *they do not know his laws.*

Still more pointedly, in Amos 3:2 God says to Israel:

'*You only have I chosen of all the families of the earth.*'
The emphasis on Israel is unmistakable and repeated constantly.

Yet that truth is not the whole truth. A little earlier we referred to Genesis 12, but the Bible does not begin with Genesis 12. There were men and women of God, who were not Israelites, before that. It could well be Adam and Eve were restored by God to himself after the trauma of the Fall and their acute sense of what they had lost. We do not know; but *somehow* their children knew of God and his requirements. Abel was godly, and so were Enoch and Noah. Melchizedek was a believing contemporary of Abraham (Genesis 14).

The promises God made to Abraham extended beyond his literal descendants. God said to him: '. . . all peoples on earth will be blessed through you' (Genesis 12:3; compare Genesis 17). To a degree this promise was realized in Old Testament times, as we shall see shortly.

Then there were a kind of 'associate' Israelites in the Old Testament period, people who not only enjoyed equal privileges with Israel, but in certain cases were actually reckoned as God's people. Moses' father-in-law, Jethro, may be described in this way (Exodus 18). Joseph's two sons by an Egyptian wife became the ancestors of two of the twelve tribes of Israel (Genesis 41:50-52, 48:1-5). Think about the harlot and liar, Rahab of Jericho (Joshua, chapters 2 and 6), and the startlingly different Ruth, a fine woman from neighbouring Moab. Both became closely linked with Israel, and, besides that, actually shared the honour of being ancestresses of Jesus Christ (Matthew 1:5)! Job, who lived presumably after Abraham's day, was probably not a Jew, but knew God as few people ever have done. Beside these specific and notable examples there is a clear emphasis in the Old Testament on God's concern

27

for the welfare of the alien, as well as of the orphan and widow (Exodus 12:48, 22:21; Psalm 146:9).

Actually there are a number of Old Testament passages, very many of them in the Psalms, that reach out far beyond Israel to the whole world. Psalm 96 begins:

> Sing to the Lord a new song;
> sing to the Lord *all the earth*.

The next Psalm starts with rejoicing because of God's dominion, and urges a response from 'the earth', even its 'distant shores'. Psalm 98:2 says, 'The Lord has made his salvation known and revealed his righteousness to the nations', while in Psalm 100 glad praise is to be offered to God by 'all the earth'. Such an attitude is impossible for those merely subject to him, and so *has* to imply *willing* submission by the world's peoples, God's people in *and beyond* Israel.

It seems that even in Old Testament times the people of God are to be seen, at least ideally, in every place and not just within the confines of national Israel. There are enough exceptions to militate against a simple Old Testament/New Testament dichotomy. It is not only Israelites who are God's people in the days of the Old Testament.

What of the New Testament? Is there any hint of a privileged Jewish position, or has that vanished without trace? Superficially there is evidence for it. In Matthew 10 the record of Jesus sending out the Twelve appears. They were not sent to Gentile or Samaritan areas, but only 'to the lost sheep of Israel'. In Romans 9:4-5 Paul describes the privileges of ancient Israel: 'Theirs is the adoption as sons; theirs the divine glory, the covenants, the receiving of the law, the temple worship and the promises. Theirs are the patriarchs, and from them is traced the human ancestry of Christ, who is God over all, for ever praised!'

The other side of the coin is seen in Peter's first letter, which is addressed to Gentile converts to Christianity: 'Once you were *not* a people, but now you *are* the people of God; once you had *not* received mercy, but now you *have* received mercy' (1 Peter 2:10; compare 4:3-4).

It is obvious that the Matthew 10 situation is temporary. At the end of the same Gospel the Great Commission is set forth with unequalled clarity and power. The regular New Testament pattern is summarized in Acts 1:8; *first* the Jews, *then* their near neighbours, *and then* people of other parts of the world. The blueprint was followed in the rest of the Acts record, and down to the present day.

A corollary of all this is that the Jews and the Gentiles are in exactly the same position before God. *All* have sinned, Jew and Gentile, as Paul tells us in Romans, chapters 1 to 3. Likewise salvation for both is found in Christ alone (Romans 3:27-31). He has 'destroyed the barrier, the dividing wall of hostility' between Jew and non-Jew (Ephesians 2:14). There are not three kinds of people now in God's purposes — Jew, Christian and non-Christian. There are only two — Christian and non-Christian. Jews appear in both groups. Gentiles appear in both. That is the burden of Romans 4 (which deserves the closest scrutiny). Paul there contends that Abraham is the spiritual father of all believers. It is spiritual likeness to him and not literal descent that is important. In Galatians 3:28 the same apostle says: 'There is neither Jew nor Greek.' Even apparent exceptions to this rule refer to priority of blessings, not to priority in the kingdom (see Romans 2:10).

The final situation is expressed incomparably in Revelation 7:9-10, where the apostle John declares:

29

After this I looked and there before me was a great multitude that no one could count, from every nation, tribe, people and language, standing before the throne and in front of the Lamb. They were wearing white robes and were holding palm branches in their hands. And they cried out in a loud voice:

'Salvation belongs to our God,
who sits on the throne,
and to the Lamb.'

5
The mistake about —
the purposes of God

The topic in this chapter forms a couplet with that of chapter 4, in that many today believe that Old Testament teaching is nationalistic and exclusive, and that God's purposes in the earlier period are confined to Israel. Later, they think, God adapted that scheme radically to include Gentiles. In other words, the Old Testament God is a Jewish God, but the New Testament God is a missionary God. Is this so?

To answer the question it is essential to see whether or not the Old Testament has a missionary thrust of an international sort. To some extent the question has been answered in our previous chapter, but here more emphasis must be placed upon God's declared purposes for mankind.

In one sense Abel was a missionary to Cain. He demonstrated God's character by doing 'what is right' (Genesis 4:7). Noah was 'a preacher of righteousness' to the people of his day (2 Peter 2:5). God declared that Abraham was to be a means of blessing 'to all peoples on earth' (Genesis 12:3), a promise partly fulfilled in the Old Testament period, though it reached its climax in the coming of Jesus Christ. In the case of Jonah, God actually required him to go as a missionary. Jonah's

was being sent to foreigners,
�…tal Assyrians! And, to his
…nted in droves, giving up 'their
…ence' (Jonah 3:8).
…t to finish extols God in glorious
… unmistakable missionary flavour.
…desire (which is *God's* great desire) is
…les' might know God's salvation and
pr… … international aspect is emphasized by
the us… …ics in the following quotation of the
Psalm:

> May God be gracious to us and bless us
> and make his face shine upon us;   *Selah*
> may your ways be known on earth,
> your salvation *among all nations*.
> May *the peoples* praise you, O God;
> may *all the peoples* praise you.
> May *the nations* be glad and sing for joy,
> for you rule *the peoples* justly
> and guide *the nations of the earth*.   *Selah*
> May *the peoples* praise you, O God;
> may *all the peoples* praise you.
> Then the land will yield its harvest,
> and God, our God, will bless us.
> God will bless us,
> and *all the ends of the earth* will fear him.

The enigmatic 'Suffering Servant' of Isaiah, who is so
easily identified with Jesus, will 'bring justice to the nations'. This justice will not be only condemnation, for
'in his law the islands *will put their hope*' (Isaiah 42:1-4).
The Servant anticipates the outreach of the New Testament church. He will be 'a light *for the Gentiles*' to
'bring . . . salvation *to the ends of the earth*' (Isaiah
49:6). Isaiah 53:12 puts it in anticipation: 'he bore the

sin of many.' While the *fulfilment* may hav
future, the promise occurs in the Old Testament.
harmony between the Testaments is again dem
strated.

When we come to the Gospels we find evidence of
missionary work based on the pre-New Testament situation. We do not usually think of the Pharisees as being
exactly outgoing in missionary ventures! Yet it is to
them that the Master said: 'You travel over land and sea
to win a single convert' (Matthew 23:15).

The so-called 'God-fearers' in the Gospel narratives,
people who had somehow sought for or been sought by
Judaism, should be noted as well. One exceptional example of this type was the centurion of Matthew 8, who
of course was a Roman. Of him Jesus declared: 'I tell
you the truth, I have not found anyone in Israel with
such great faith.' The Ethiopian of Acts 8 and the centurion of Acts 10 were two more notable cases. They
were both foreign 'God-fearers'. So, of course, had
been many of those who crowded Jerusalem at Pente-
cost (Acts 2:9-11).

The missionary aspect of God's purposes may be approached from quite a different direction. In Exodus
19:5-6 God says to Israel: 'Now if you obey me fully . . .
then *out of all nations* you will be my treasured posses-
sion. *Although the whole earth is mine*, you will be for
me *a kingdom of priests* and a holy nation.' One writer
has interpreted this to mean that all of Israel served as
'Levites to the nations', that is, the Israelites were to be
a vehicle of blessing to others. The twelve tribes, chosen
and blessed by the Lord, were to be a missionary
spearhead. A possible parallel may be seen in the
Gospels. Jesus 'appointed twelve . . . that they might be
with him [chosen and blessed] and that he might send
them out to preach [missionary outreach]' (see Mark

33

been

Thus

text).

ses — insofar as they are revealed in at root *one* purpose: *the manifestation f God through achieving salvation in* . This theme of salvation is to be r next chapter. Both Testaments testify to it.

6
The mistake about —
salvation

A point of view that flourishes all over Christendom is that in the Old Testament personal salvation comes by observing the law, but in the New Testament by trusting in Christ. Put rather differently, the contrast is between salvation by works and salvation by grace. This, however, is far from being the case and betrays a gross misunderstanding of the Old Testament.

The subject can best be approached by first considering the New Testament.

In the teaching of Jesus and the apostles three over-arching terms are used to describe the basic good that God does in a person's life. One is *to enter the kingdom of God*. The concept of the kingdom is common in the first three Gospels, rare in John (but not absent from it; see 3:1-5), and fairly frequent in the rest of the New Testament. John prefers a second expression: that of *gaining eternal life*. Particularly noteworthy examples are John 3:15, 5:40, 6:68, 10:28 and 17:2-3, while Matthew 19:16 and 25:46 are fine instances from another Gospel. The third term is *salvation* itself, or *being saved*. Before we go further, we need to be very clear that this salvation is not a deliverance from ignorance in the first instance, and still less a deliverance from any current physical danger, but it is rescue *from sin*. The fact is luminous in the statement that 'Christ Jesus came into the world *to save sinners*' (1 Timothy 1:15).

Salvation is a very rich term that has several distinct elements. In Jesus' teaching, a person must be *convicted* of his sin (John 16:8). Closely associated with conviction is spiritual *rebirth*, an activity ascribed to the Holy Spirit in John 3:1-8. The proper human response to God's work is stated in almost identical ways by John the Baptist and Jesus: '*Repent and believe* the good news!' (Mark 1:15; compare 1:4). Such a heartfelt response, involving a renunciation of sin and a deep commitment to God, is invariably joined to divine *forgiveness* (Luke 7:44-50).

But neither faith nor forgiveness may be regarded in isolation. *Everything* for man's salvation *is centred on Jesus himself*. He declared: '*I* am the way and the truth and the life. No one comes to the Father except through me' (John 14:6). To be more precise still, we need to realize that salvation depends on Jesus' *death*. That death is *substitutionary* — his death in the place of others. So vital are these things, that, in order to avoid misunderstanding, we give a few key Gospel verses.

Talking of himself, Jesus said: 'I tell you the truth, unless an ear of wheat falls to the ground and dies, it remains only a single seed. But if it dies, it produces many seeds' (John 12:24).

A little earlier he had taught: 'I am the good shepherd . . . I lay down my life for the sheep' (John 10:11-15).

He said that he actually came to earth in order to die for others: 'For even the Son of Man [= Jesus] did not come to be served, but to serve, and to give his life as a ransom for many' (Mark 10:45).

At the Last Supper Jesus referred to his 'blood of the covenant, which is poured out for many for the forgiveness of sins' (Matthew 26:28). A disciple present then later summarized Jesus' message in this way: 'For Christ died for sins once for all, the righteous for the unrighteous, to bring you to God' (1 Peter 3:18). The great apostle Paul used different words to convey the same message: 'Christ redeemed us from the curse of the law by becoming a curse for us' (Galatians 3:13).

One other crucial term occurs in the Gospels (Luke 18:14), but is more common in the other New Testament writings. That is *justification*, the fact of sinners being acquitted at the bar of God because of the saving death of Jesus. Paul writes to the Romans: '. . . all have sinned and fall short of the glory of God, and are justified freely by his grace through the redemption that came by Christ Jesus' (Romans 3:23-24).

That reference to 'grace' brings us full circle, back to where the chapter began. The New Testament teaches salvation *by grace*. Salvation is not by works: 'For *it is by grace you have been saved* through faith — and this not from yourselves, it is the gift of God — *not by works*, so that no-one can boast' (Ephesians 2:8-9).

When we turn back to the earlier Testament, we find anticipations of the key ideas. *The kingdom of God* is seen in Psalms 103:19 and 145:11-13 and in Daniel 2:44 and 4:3. *Eternal life* is at least suggested in Job 19:26 and explicitly proclaimed in Daniel 12:2. *Salvation* occurs over and over again in the Old Testament, more than forty of the instances being in the Psalms and Isaiah. Most passages employ the word in a military or other physical sense, but that is hardly true of Isaiah 12:3 and 45:17, and certainly not of Isaiah 52:10 and 61:10. The necessity for *repentance* and *trust* in God is like a thread running through the Old Testament, a thread which cannot be ignored even by the most casual reader. And so we could go on, adducing parallels

37

between the Old and the New Testaments. But that is hardly necessary. Paul has done the task for us.

In Genesis 15:6 we read: 'Abram [= Abraham] believed the Lord, and he credited it to him as righteousness.' In Romans 4 Paul demonstrates that this verse is crucial for an understanding of salvation in both Testaments. Abraham could *not* justify himself by works — that would have been boasting; and God, who does not change, surely did not approve of boasting before Christ came any more than he does now! (See Malachi 3:6; James 1:17; Romans 4:1-3; Ephesians 2:8-9.) Abraham was justified through trusting in God, who *could* justify him. Like all others who are saved, he trusted 'God who justifies the wicked' (Romans 4:5). Besides, Abraham could not possibly have been justified by keeping the law, explains Paul in Romans 4:13 and Galatians 3:6-9,17, for the law was not given until more than four hundred years later! Nor was he acquitted before God by some rite such as circumcision, because even that came years after the statement of Genesis 15:6 (see Romans 4:9-10; compare Genesis 17).

Paul writes of Israel's greatest king in a similar way. 'David . . . speaks of the blessedness of the man to whom God credits *righteousness apart from works*.' This is followed in Romans 4 by a quotation from Psalm 32. David's plea in Psalm 51 for forgiveness and cleansing from sin is based solely on God's mercy (which approximately equals his grace). The psalmist specifically acknowledges that ceremonial observances will not meet his case. Corresponding with the mercy of God is the humble contrition of the sinner:

> The sacrifices of God are a broken spirit;
> a broken and contrite heart,
> O God, you will not despise (v. 17).

Isaiah 53 is climactic. After a graphic portrayal of the humble circumstances of the incarnate Son of God, Isaiah writes of the substitutionary vocation of Jesus Christ, of his bearing the sins of others, of his being punished for them:

> Surely *he took up our infirmities*
>   and *carried our sorrows*,
> yet we considered him stricken by God,
>   smitten by him, and afflicted.
> But *he was pierced for our transgressions,*
>   *he was crushed for our iniquities;*
> *the punishment that brought us peace was upon him,*
>   and *by his wounds we are healed.*
> We all, like sheep, have gone astray,
>   each of us has turned to his own way;
> *and the Lord has laid on him the iniquity of us all.*
>   (Isaiah 53:4-6)

Because Jesus was afflicted he 'will justify many' (v. 11). In other words, they will be saved by his suffering and through their commitment to him, not by works. Eight chapters later the same glorious facts are spelled out in a symbolic fashion:

> I delight greatly in the Lord;
>   my soul rejoices in my God.
> For he has clothed me with garments of salvation
>   and arrayed me in a robe of righteousness.
>   (Isaiah 61:10; compare Matthew 22:1-14
>   and Revelation 7:9.)

Jeremiah also refers to 'The Lord Our Righteousness' (23:6, 33:16). We are accounted righteous through him, through the Lord.

Righteousness is not achieved by works then, but is a gift of God. How could it ever be otherwise? If I could keep the law from now on, how would that deal with either my sinful nature (1 John 1:8; compare Romans 7:14-25) or with my past acts of sin (1 John 1:10)? Surely only Adam and Eve were ever in a state where God's favour could be enjoyed by means of 'works'. Even then they had to continue in a right relationship to God, an attitude of unquestioning trust that would not lead to sin. God *never* promised to anyone else salvation by works.

But surely God gave the law for a purpose? Was it not meant to be kept? The answer to both questions is in the affirmative, but that does not mean that the law is the instrument of salvation. The purposes of the law were in the realms of *teaching* and the *regulation of life*. In the first respect the law showed people what God is like. It demonstrated his righteousness, holiness and sublimity. It taught, too, what God requires of humankind. It taught by implication that beyond its own inadequacy (at least in its cultic aspects; see Hebrews 9:1-15) God had One who is always perfectly adequate. In short, salvation is *always* through Christ, even though the Old Testament believer saw him only dimly and intermittently (John 8:56, 12:41; for a general summary see Galatians 3:11).

At the moral level the law, especially the Ten Commandments, was given to be regulative of conduct. It was intended to restrain wickedness and to promote goodness. By attending to both these emphases people would be guided aright.

Because it was God-given, the law must never be viewed as evil, but as 'holy, righteous and good' (Romans 7:12). Men have imposed upon it a purpose it was never intended to serve. We must not try to make the law do what God denounces.

7
The mistake about — religion

Many Christians affirm that Old Testament religion is *external* and material while New Testament religion is *internal* and spiritual. There seems to be some basis for the view if one is very selective in the choice of material. Jeremiah apparently supports the contention in his thirty-first chapter. The whole pronouncement of God from verse 31 to verse 34 should be read, but particularly that part of the prophecy where God promises:

> I will put my law *in their minds*
> and write it *on their hearts*.

Ezekiel also highlights the inwardness of the new covenant in 36:26, where he too quotes the Lord: 'I will give you a new heart and *put a new spirit in you*; I will remove from you your heart of stone and give you a heart of flesh.' In both of these prophecies the quality of inwardness *is* stressed with regard to the new covenant. However, the contrast is not between the new situation envisaged by the prophets and the old situation as God intended it to be. It is a contrast with *bad* examples from the earlier era.

Let us try to survey some central aspects of Old Testament religion to see how the general situation is presented. A similar treatment of other aspects would yield a like result.

First we consider the Ten Commandments in Exodus 20. Some of these look like edicts that do not touch the heart, but which are to be obeyed almost in the way a robot might comply with an order. The second commandment prohibits the making of idols, the third blasphemy, the fourth desecration of the Sabbath, the fifth dishonouring parents, and later ones deal with murder, adultery, theft and lying. But let us go a little more deeply. The first commandment follows an exercise in reflection. God has done *this*, and *this* — *therefore* — *obey the commandments*. The first two demand the inward attitude of loyalty to the God of Israel. The last is a genuinely inward instruction, while several others demand careful consideration of the consequences of obedience and disobedience.

Inevitably our minds move towards *the sacrificial system* as we start to think about Old Testament worship. This elaborate series of rituals may strike the reader as mechanical, but that conclusion is false. 'Mechanical' religion is an *abuse* of the Levitical system, not the *use* of it. Look at the evidence: in instance after instance the offering is described as 'without defect' (e.g. Leviticus 1:3,10; 3:1,6; 4:3). Why without defect? Because God commands it. Why does he command it? Because he is without defect himself and — something the ordinary Old Testament worshipper could not be expected to know — because it anticipates the perfection of Christ's self-sacrifice (Hebrews 9:14). The worshipper was to *think*! He was often to *identify* himself with the proffered animal victim by laying his hand on its head (see Leviticus 1:4, 4:4). Identification is particularly important in Leviticus 16, that great chapter on the Day of Atonement.

The third Old Testament feature of religion we need to look at is that of *prayer*. Now prayer is very common in the Old Testament. The first extended prayer (really a series of prayers) is in Genesis 18, where Abraham pleads with God for Sodom. There are almost endless examples from the life of Moses, from the Psalms, from Nehemiah's brief book, and there are extraordinarily important instances in the story of Daniel (2:17-19, and chapters 6 and 9). Prayer cannot possibly be conceived of as an 'external' activity, though it may be accompanied by certain physical postures of a distinctive sort.

Related to prayer is worship that centres on *conversations with God*. Apart from Abraham and Moses there are the prophets, especially Isaiah, Jeremiah and Ezekiel. Isaiah's commissioning in the temple by God is the supreme example, but there are similar circumstances elsewhere, accompanied in Ezekiel's case by a like overwhelming vision (see Isaiah chapter 6, Jeremiah chapter 1 and Ezekiel chapters 1 and 2). Who would dare to call *these* experiences 'external'?

Next, there is *singing and instrumental music*, sometimes spontaneous and sometimes a planned production by a properly constituted choir or orchestra. An informal song is the famous 'Song of Moses' of Deuteronomy 32. David organized both choirs and instrumentalists, we are told in 1 Chronicles 15:16-22. The Psalms themselves are the hymn-book of Israel. Some Psalms, notably the last, contain instructions regarding the use of music in worship. Of course one can sing or play a musical instrument without necessarily engaging in spiritual worship, but again that is a parody, not the intention of God.

Most important of all, there is the *call-and-commitment* theme in the Old Testament. Isaiah, Jeremiah and Ezekiel are mentioned above, but what of the call of Moses (Exodus, chapters 3 and 4)? This exchange between God and men seems something basic to all true religion. We could work backward to Abraham and Noah, or forward to Samuel, David, Amos and hosts of others. The whole people of Israel is involved in, for example, Exodus 19. Is *this* activity *external*? Proverbs 21:2-3 provides a summary of true Old Testament religion:

> All a man's ways seem right to him,
>   but the Lord weighs the heart.
> To do what is right and just
>   is more acceptable to the Lord than sacrifice.

Israel's religion, then, was to engage the mind and the heart. Otherwise expressed, it was to be essentially *inward*, though there was often corresponding outward ritual. Indeed, Jesus' complaint about the teachers of the law and the Pharisees was that they had perverted God-given religion *by* externalizing it. They had also trivialized it. For these two sins they are roundly condemned by Jesus in the terrible 'seven woes' of Matthew 23.

Sometimes *New Testament* religion could be described superficially as 'external'. The two sacraments given by Jesus, baptism and the Lord's Supper, are both 'ceremonies'. Yet surely no one can read Matthew 28:19-20, Acts 8:26-40 or Colossians 2:9-12 prayerfully and still think baptism is only external. John 6 gives the inner meaning of the Lord's Supper in very clear terms, and 1 Corinthians 11:17-34 contains a number of consequences of the observance of the rite. These are in the areas of devotion, thought, confession and conduct.

Other 'outward' aspects of the Christian religion portrayed in the New Testament are almsgiving, or looking after the practical needs of widows and others in want (see, for example, Acts 6, James 2:14-17 and 1 John 3:17-18), and the provision of hospitality for faithful itinerant teachers (3 John). (Conversely, hospitality is, as 2 John makes clear, to be refused to the heretical teacher, so that his venom does not spread.) The fatherless, underprivileged and imprisoned are to be visited and aided (Matthew 25; Hebrews 13). Christians in fact are to 'spur one another on towards love and good deeds' (Hebrews 10:24).

Are these things any less 'external' than many Old Testament instructions?

There is no biblical evidence that God ever intended people's religion to be *merely* external. The idea is preposterous, a contradiction. All worship and God-centred living that has an exterior aspect has an interior one as well.

Where, then, did the commonly held notion come from?

There are two passages that have a bearing on the subject. One is the Sermon on the Mount. In his teaching there, Jesus emphasized the place of the mind and the will in sin, as an antidote to misunderstandings which were then current. Thus, hatred is the parent of murder, lust of adultery and so on. Such sinful attitudes were condemned by him even if they never led on to the act. Jesus therefore showed the ramifications and consequences of the commandments, that guilt was incurred before the sins were actually committed. The commands were simply more sharply etched by him. He did not come to displace the Old with something different here: 'Do not think that I have come to abolish the Law or the Prophets; I have not come to abolish them but to fulfil them' (Matthew 5:17). The chapter concerned demands meticulous scrutiny here.

The other New Testament passage of surpassing

importance is Hebrews, especially chapter 9. 'The blood of goats and bulls and the ashes of a heifer' might make one 'outwardly clean'. In the sharpest possible contrast, 'the blood of Christ' can '*cleanse our consciences*' (Hebrews 9:13,14)! But was not that always so? Abraham and David reckoned it so. So did Isaiah (see chapter 53). So did Paul! So did God (Genesis 15:6; Romans 4)!

But someone may say at this point: 'The very passage that you just quoted — Hebrews 9 — goes on to talk about a "new covenant" as well as "the first covenant". Are you saying that there is no difference?' No, but it must be remembered that the 'new covenant' really predates the covenant of Sinai! We remind ourselves again that Paul's fourth chapter to the Romans is devoted to the subject. (In another connection also Jesus goes back to the intention of God prior to Sinai and regards it as the ideal state of affairs — see Matthew 19:1-12.)

In essence of course both Old Testament and New Testament religion are primarily internal because both are related to Christ and his salvation. Basically, therefore, they are one, but represent different stages of revelation and realization.

8
The mistake about —
godly living

A familiar misconception surrounds the pattern of life set out in the Bible. Put in contrasting fashion, it goes like this: 'In the Old Testament God requires obedience to commandments as the way of life, but in the New Testament the Christian, saved by grace, is free from commandments.'

Such a simplistic view is utterly false. Like some of the other popular notions we have examined, it disintegrates in the face of what Scripture says. We will proceed here by way of question and answer.

First, *does the Old Testament contain commandments for the Lord's people*? Plainly, the answer to such a question can only be, 'Yes!' In the book of Exodus, for instance, there are commands of a *personal* sort. Think of God's call to Moses in chapters 3 and 4 (see 3:5,10,15,16,18, 4:3, etc.). Similar instructions to an individual person are multiplied on the pages of Scripture as God calls his chosen servants and sends them off on their task or vocation. Other examples are found in the call of priests (Exodus 28:1-3) and prophets (1 Kings 19:16) and kings (1 Samuel 16:1-13). Sometimes God's commands relate to *a temporary situation* in the life of a people, particularly (but not necessarily) Israel. The special instructions surrounding the first Passover (Exodus 12), the crossing of the Red Sea and the wilderness itinerary of Exodus and Numbers, are properly described in this fashion. The detailed scheme for the tabernacle is also a 'one-off' matter, important as it was to be in Israelite life. The ceremonial law of Leviticus consisted of a series of commands *for prolonged observance*. By contrast, some words of God are literally *for all time*. The Ten Commandments are of this kind (Exodus 20). Indeed, surely the first commandment is not just for all time, but *for all eternity* as well. Such a message of God is even more than that, though, for surely it applies to all of God's higher creation, including angels and other exalted beings (Revelation 4).

Secondly, *what kind of commands do we find in Old Testament religion?* If we now confine ourselves to the heartland of religion, we find five kinds of God-given instruction in the Old Testament. There are *hygienic* laws such as those relating to personal cleanliness or to medical conditions (Leviticus 11; compare Leviticus chapters 13 to 15 and Numbers 19:11-14). Sometimes the hygienic is scarcely distinguishable from the *ceremonial* law, as in Exodus 30:17-21 and Numbers 19. Other ceremonial laws are distinct, as is seen in the descriptions of Leviticus 23 about the way to observe 'the Lord's appointed feasts'. *Social* and *moral* commandments include prohibitions on sexual relations of an incestuous kind (Leviticus 18), adultery and theft (Exodus 20). The greatest social command occurs in Leviticus 19:18, 'Love your neighbour as yourself.' '*Cultic* commandments' is a suitable title for the regulation governing the offering of the various sacrifices (see especially Leviticus, chapters 1 to 7). *Theological* commands include the demand of unswerving loyalty to God alone (Exodus 20:3). The high point is Deuteronomy

48

6:4-5: 'Hear, O Israel: The Lord our God, the Lord is one. Love the Lord your God with all your heart and with all your soul and with all your strength.' Obviously there is overlap here and other classifications may be quite as good or even preferable. Nevertheless, some idea of the life-embracing range of God's commandments in the Old Testament is apparent from our very brief analysis.

Thirdly, *are there God-given commandments in the New Testament*? Most definitely! Old Testament laws are repeated in Matthew 5, Romans 7 and elsewhere. There are *ceremonial* commands, such as those concerning the sacraments. Jesus said: 'make disciples . . . *baptising* them in the name of the Father and of the Son and of the Holy Spirit' (Matthew 28:19). In 1 Corinthians 11:23, Paul says that he 'received from the Lord' the words of institution for the Supper and, in that, he closely follows the instructions of Jesus recorded in the first three Gospels. *Social* and *moral* commands are quite as common in the New Testament as in the Old. In this connection, homosexuality is roundly censured in Romans 1, and adultery in Hebrews 13:4 and in the seven letters of Revelation (chapters 2 and 3). Even association with the incestuous is forbidden — that is, with the *Christian* or at least professing Christian who is guilty of this sin (1 Corinthians 5:1-11). The Epistle of James is very clear on the need to correct social evils. The provision of hospitality and the visiting of the prisoner are virtual commands in Hebrews 13. More broadly, the writer of that letter says 'Keep on loving each other as brothers', which is a restatement of the 'new commandment' of John 13:34. Jesus prohibits hatred and lust (Matthew 5). The Christian is to obey the laws of the land (Romans 13:1-7), though he is fundamentally subject to a still higher law (Matthew 22:21).

Jesus' teaching on the kingdom is important. He is the King, a truth that necessarily involves obedience on the part of his subjects. In a similar way he is called 'Master' (Ephesians 6:9). The obedient follower is not *only* a subject, but on the ground of his obedience to Jesus' commands, is honoured with the title 'friend' (John 15:14).

Theologically, the Christian, the person who has been raised to a new life spiritually with Christ, is commanded to have his affections firmly set 'on things above, where Christ is seated at the right hand of God' (Colossians 3:1; compare Matthew 6:33). Idolatry is utterly abhorrent to God, says the New Testament as well as the Old (Romans 1). God is to be loved unreservedly, and this is without doubt the greatest of all commandments (Mark 12:28-31).

Fourthly, *how does the New Testament differ from the Old Testament in this matter of commandments*?

Some old commands are quite definitely rescinded. Both Peter and Paul, following their Master, came to the point of understanding that Levitical food-laws were no longer operative — nor were ceremonial washings (see Matthew 15 and compare Acts 10 and Romans 14:20). No physical sacrifices are to be offered in the Christian era because Jesus himself was the sacrifice to end all sacrifices. Any notion that animal or food sacrifices will ever be legitimately offered again is a blasphemy, for it denies the 'once-for-allness' of Jesus' self-sacrifice (Hebrews 9:12-14, 10:11-13). Then there is a new intensity about the commands of the second Testament, and a wider application of them. Unjustified anger is prohibited along with murder, lust with adultery and so on. Positively, one is to love not only one's neighbour, but even one's enemy (Matthew 5).

The power of an example is more prominent in the

New Testament. Jesus' followers are to model themselves on him in humility and in readiness to serve (John 13:1-17; Philippians 2:1-11) as well as in submission to abuse (1 Peter 2:23). Christian leaders likewise are to be of such a character that others can follow them confidently (Philippians 3:17; Hebrews 13:7). Love is enjoined more often in the New Testament, being in fact *the* characteristic in the present era (John 13:34-35; but see Leviticus 19:18 and Deuteronomy 6:4-5). The shortest book in the New Testament expresses it so succinctly, and in the process comes full circle in this matter of commandments:

> I am not writing you a new command but one we have had from the beginning. I ask that we love one another. And this is love: that we walk in obedience to his commands. As you have heard from the beginning, his command is that you walk in love (2 John 5-6).

Before ending this chapter we ought to ask and answer another basic question: *What is the purpose of the commandments, and of the Ten Commandments in particular?*

Paul says forthrightly: 'Clearly no-one is justified before God by the law, because "The righteous will live by faith"' (Galatians 3:11). No one becomes a child of God by keeping his laws, whether he lived before or after Christ's coming. (That was the subject we dealt with in chapter 6.) Amongst things the law does are the following:

It shows what God is like. His holiness and purity are demonstrated in what he demands (1 Peter 1:15-16).

It shows what God requires of his people.

It shows man his inability to obey God apart from Christ (Romans 3:23).

It therefore acts as a signpost, pointing beyond itself to Jesus Christ (Galatians 3:24).

It teaches through the sacrificial system about the nature of Christ's work (Hebrews 10:1-10).

The law is vital. God requires obedience to his commands. That is what the gospel is about. God is exalted and pure in his character. Man, made in his image, fell into sin. In other words, he became disobedient. He could not then retrieve the situation. *Jesus* retrieved it. How? He did two things. One was *to render the obedience* to God that we did not render — he obeyed God's laws. 'I always do what pleases him,' he said (John 8:29). The other was *to pay the penalty for the disobedience* of men and women (1 Peter 3:18). He suffered for our failure to obey God's laws. This is what Paul means when he says that '*Christ is the end of the law* so that there may be righteousness for everyone who believes' (Romans 10:4). He is 'the end' in the sense that he put an end to hopes of justification by law-keeping. He is also the 'end' of the law in that he realized or fulfilled it.

The basic purpose of God's commands is that he may be honoured by their being kept (John 14:15). His law is not arbitrary, for it expresses his character. The one who keeps the commands is therefore becoming increasingly like his God (1 Peter 1:16). Finally, through the operations of the Holy Spirit (2 Corinthians 3:18), the child of God will be like Christ (1 John 3:2).

9
The difference between the Old and New Testaments

Every one of the eight mistakes about the Bible which we have examined in this book results in a distortion of the Christian faith. In some instances the distortion is so severe that the Faith itself becomes unrecognizable.

There is an indissoluble and vital link between the Testaments. They have an internal harmony that reflects the consistency of God's own perfect nature (Malachi 3:6). Perhaps, though, our insistence on this has given the impression that there is no essential difference between the Old Testament and the New Testament.

There are many important differences between the Testaments. Here we can highlight only a few, but all of them of such magnitude that they should never be overlooked.

The Old Testament begins with the account of creation. God, the triune God, was alone before time or anything else existed. Then he created the unseen world and angels, the cosmos with its astounding forces, its inanimate phenomena, its plant and animal life, and man. Both Testaments affirm that God created all that is (apart from himself) by his word (Psalm 33:6; John 1:1-3; Hebrews 11:3), but the Old Testament provides far more detail. Creation is not just the first among God's acts, but the great prior miracle that is unique.

The Old Testament also contains the record of the Fall of man, without which the New Testament would be meaningless. The bad news must be understood and proclaimed before the Good News can be preached!

Unlike the New Testament, the Old supplies us with totally persuasive historical evidence of the sovereignty of God in the affairs of nations and empires, and that over centuries. Babylon, Egypt, Assyria, Babylon (again) and Persia rise, thrive and fall at his unchallengeable command. His hand is seen even more clearly in the changing fortunes of Israel and Judah.

The Old Testament contains a repository of hymnody and prayer in its poetic books (especially the Psalms) that has no peer or parallel.

Equally clearly there are New Testament distinctives. One is the incomparable clarity of the gospel presentation in its pages. It was only after the Son of God became manifest that people — even people prepared by God — could appreciate the full vista of the gospel.

In the first four books of the New Testament we read of the incarnation and its consequences. God became man, the Word became flesh, for us and our salvation. The Gospels of course also record the ministry of Jesus, his crucifixion, burial, resurrection and ascension.

The New Testament does not consist merely of Gospels, though, but portrays the practical outworking of the gospel in Acts, and includes the explication of the gospel in the Epistles. Put otherwise, after the Preparation (the Old Testament), we have the Manifestation (the Gospel records), the Propagation (Acts), the Explanation (the Epistles) and the Consummation (the book of Revelation).

That last point needs further comment. Just as the Old Testament deals with the story of the beginnings of humankind in the bright light of Eden before the Fall, so the New Testament ends with 'Paradise (actually) Regained'. The book of Revelation is the story of the victory of the kingly Son of God and his people. Just as the New Testament lacks a beginning, the Old lacks a climax!

The New Testament repeatedly tells of the inauguration of the new covenant which supersedes as well as in a sense precedes the Sinai covenant (see chapter 6 above). The God-given covenant of Sinai bound his people to him in terms of blessing or judgment on his side and loyalty and obedience on theirs. The new covenant, foretold by Jeremiah and Ezekiel, found expression at the Last Supper and in 1 Corinthians chapter 11, realization at the cross, and explanation in Hebrews 8 and 9. That covenant has a superior Mediator (Christ instead of Moses) and 'better promises'. It involves a true, eternal and complete cleansing from sin because it is centred on the self-sacrifice of Jesus Christ as a substitute and ransom for men and women (Hebrews 9:15; Galatians 3:13; 1 Peter 3:18).

The New Testament reveals Jesus as Intercessor for his people. He is the believer's Advocate in heaven, as the Holy Spirit has become his Advocate on earth (Hebrews 7:25; 1 John 2:1; John 14:16,17,26).

The Testaments differ with respect to prophecies too. If we were to simplify a complex subject, we could say that the Old Testament prophecies are *prospective*, that is, for the most part they anticipate a fulfilment of New Testament times. The fulfilment is most frequently centred on Jesus the Christ (see Genesis 3:15, Deuteronomy

18:15, Psalm 22, Isaiah 42, 53 and so on). The New Testament shows prophecies *fulfilled* in the life and ministry of Jesus, and particularly in his death. (See the marginal references to Old Testament passages beside the Gospel accounts of the Passion.) Further, the New Testament contains prophecies uttered by Jesus and fulfilled in his own life-time (Mark 8:31, 9:31, 10:32-34), and prophecies yet to be consummated since they relate to the Lord's *second* coming (Matthew 24:27-31; John 14:1-3; Acts 1:10-11; 1 Thessalonians 4:16; Hebrews 9:28). Thus the Bible goes full circle with respect to its primary subject, God's Son:

Heaven — earth — heaven — earth

Our approach to the Bible has helped us to discern something of the glorious panorama of God's dealings with man in the book's 'roundedness' and completeness. May we see the hand of God at work as we study both parts of God's authoritative revelation, a revelation which begins in a garden and (for his people) ends with a garden. In thinking of this prospect may our earnest wish be to be present with him! May we strive to live God-exalting lives, aglow with expectant hope! May we echo the climactic utterance of God's aged servant, who at the end of the Bible exclaimed: 'Come, Lord Jesus' (Revelation 22:20)!

Forty years earlier a great colleague of his reached a crescendo when he cried in triumph: 'For from him and through him and to him are all things. To him be the glory for ever! Amen' (Romans 11:36).

Further reading

Anderson, J.N.D., *Jesus Christ: The Witness of History* (Leicester: IVP, 1985).

Bavinck, Herman, *The Doctrine of God*, tr. William Hendriksen (Edinburgh: Banner of Truth Trust, 1977).

Boice, James Montgomery, *Does Inerrancy Matter?* (Wheaton, Illinois: Tyndale House Publishers, 1980).

Bruce, F.F., *The New Testament Documents*, fifth edition (London: IVF, 1960).

Bruce, F.F., *The Time is Fulfilled: Five Aspects of the Fulfilment of the Old Testament in the New* (Exeter: Paternoster, 1978).

Bruce, F.F., *This is That: The New Testament Development of Some Old Testament Themes* (Exeter: Paternoster, 1968; paperback ed., 1976).

Houghton, S.M., *Sketches from Church History* (Edinburgh: Banner of Truth Trust, 1980).

Kitchen, K.A., *The Bible in its World: The Bible and Archaeology Today* (Exeter: Paternoster, 1977).

Knox, D. Broughton, *The Everlasting God* (Welwyn: Evangelical Press, 1982).

Machen, J. Gresham, *Christianity and Liberalism* (Grand Rapids, Michigan: Wm. B. Eerdmans Publishing Co., 1923).

McDonald, H.D., *Jesus — Human and Divine: An Introduction to New Testament Christology* (London & Glasgow: Pickering & Inglis, 1983).

Morris, Leon, *The Lord from Heaven* (London: IVF, 1958).

Packer, J.I. & Tenney, Merrill C., *Daily Life in Bible Times* (Nashville, Tennessee: Thomas Nelson Publishers, 1982).

Packer, J.I., *Knowing God* (London: Hodder & Stoughton, 1973).

Owen, G. Frederick, 'Archaeological Supplement', *The Holy Bible — New International Version: Thompson Chain Reference Edition* (London: Hodder & Stoughton, 1984).

Young, Edward J., *Thy Word is Truth: Some Thoughts on the Biblical Doctrine of Inspiration* (London: Banner of Truth Trust, 1963).

NOTES

CHRISTIAN HANDBOOK

by

Peter Jeffery

This new handbook provides a basic introduction to the Bible, church history and Christian doctrine. In *one* handy volume it therefore provides a range of information which would otherwise only be found either in much larger and more expensive publications, or in a large number of smaller ones. Written in a plain and straightforward style, it will prove invaluable not only for the new Christian but for all who want to broaden their knowledge of the Christian faith.

- Over 90 illustrations including maps, charts, drawings and photographs.
- A comprehensive index.
- Available in hardback and paperback.

'This is a great little handbook, the best of its kind. Let every church buy a copy for each new convert; it's just what they need' — Brian H. Edwards in *Evangelicals Now*.

'This book is packed with information that every Christian needs to know. It is an ideal handbook for young people, Christians and all who wish to broaden their knowledge of the Christian faith' — David Barker in *Grace*.

REVIVAL

Books by Dr Eifion Evans published by the Evangelical Press of Wales:

THE WELSH REVIVAL OF 1904

A thorough but very readable study of the 1904 Revival, with a foreword by Dr Martyn Lloyd-Jones.

REVIVAL COMES TO WALES

A moving and thrilling account of the mighty working of God the Holy Spirit in Wales at the time of the 1859 Revival.

REVIVALS: THEIR RISE, PROGRESS AND ACHIEVEMENTS

A general survey of revivals and their characteristics, concentrating especially on those of the eighteenth century.

TWO WELSH REVIVALISTS

The fascinating stories of Humphrey Jones and Dafydd Morgan, the two prominent leaders during the 1859 Revival in Wales.

Further titles from the Evangelical Press of Wales relating to the subject of revival:

REVIVAL AND ITS FRUIT

by Emyr Roberts & R. Geraint Gruffydd

Studies on the nature of revival and the phenomena associated with it.

HOWELL HARRIS AND THE DAWN OF REVIVAL

by Richard Bennett; introduction by
D. Martyn Lloyd-Jones

Formerly published under the title **The Early Life of Howell Harris,** this book is an invaluable study of the early spiritual life of Howell Harris and the beginnings of the Great Awakening of the eighteenth century in Wales.

CHRISTIAN HYMNS

Paul E. G. Cook and
Graham Harrison (editors)

Over 80,000 copies of *Christian Hymns* have been sold since it was first published in 1977. The warm reception given to it by both churches and the Christian press confirm the view of many that it is one of the finest hymn-books available today.

- Comprehensive selection of 900 hymns.
- Suitable for public worship and informal church gatherings.
- Include 80 metrical psalms and paraphrases.
- Useful children's section.
- Beautifully bound and printed by Oxford University Press.

Words editions	Music editions
Standard words	Standard music
De-luxe words	Presentation music
Large-type words	(with slip case)

CHRISTIAN HYMN-WRITERS

Elsie Houghton

The stories behind some of the great hymns are often as inspiring as the hymns themselves. This fascinating book takes us 'behind the scenes' and enables us to appreciate much more those words with which we are so familiar. In brief but telling biographies, the author covers a wide range of hymn-writers from the early centuries of the Christian church down to the twentieth century. This popular work comes complete with a valuable index, and has now been reprinted with a bright new cover.

Books by Dr Martyn Lloyd-Jones published by Evangelical Press of Wales:

OUT OF THE DEPTHS
This book deals with the problem of human failure and guilt and the divine remedy of repentance. The author looks at the subject in the light of Psalm 51, and shows us exactly what repentance means, and how Christians and non-Christians alike may experience new joy in their lives. This is an immensely encouraging book.

WHY DOES GOD ALLOW WAR?
Why does God seem not to answer the prayers of His people in the face of evil and suffering? In this reprint of wartime sermons Dr Lloyd-Jones deals honestly and sympathetically with this question and answers some of our misunderstandings both about the nature of God and the nature of the Christian life.

Books on contemporary issues published by Evangelical Press of Wales:

SOCIAL ISSUES AND THE LOCAL CHURCH
Ian Shaw (editor)
Among the subjects covered by this work are: the Christian and the state, the Christian concern for education, the role of women in the church, social welfare and the local church and mission in today's world.

CHRISTIAN FAMILY MATTERS
Ian Shaw (editor); foreword by Sir Frederick Catherwood
Here is clear biblical teaching by experienced contributors on marriage, parenthood, childhood and adolescence, the handicapped child, fostering and adoption, divorce, abortion and family planning, and the care of the elderly.

THE CHRISTIAN, THE CHURCH AND DAILY WORK
Gerallt Wyn Davies
In this little book the author looks at biblical teaching regarding work, compares it with society's attitudes, and outlines what individual Christians and the church could do to be of effective help in alleviating the great social problem of unemployment.